Sharpurr
the Carpet Snake

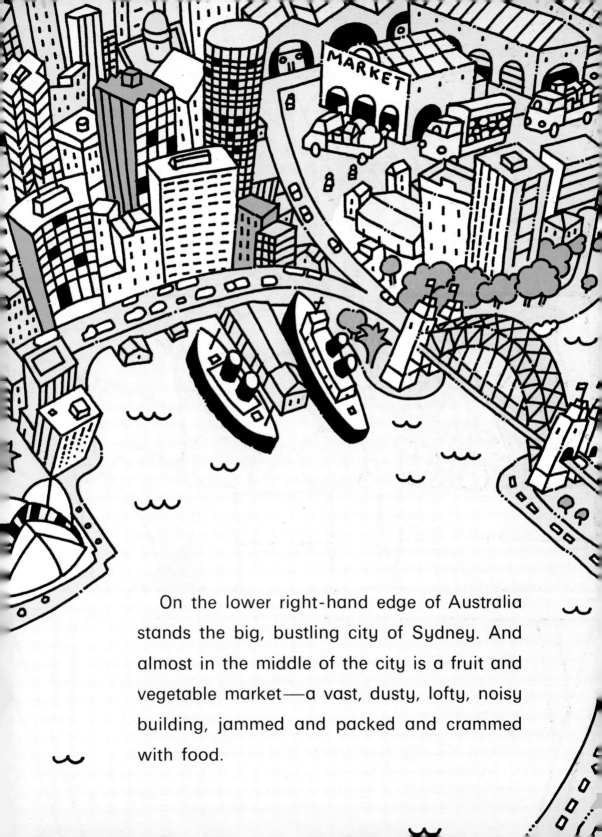

On the lower right-hand edge of Australia stands the big, bustling city of Sydney. And almost in the middle of the city is a fruit and vegetable market—a vast, dusty, lofty, noisy building, jammed and packed and crammed with food.

There are peas and persimmons and pumpkins, and beans and bananas and beetroot, and apples and artichokes and

50¢

TODAYS SPECIAL

BEANS

apricots, nailed into cases or sewn into sacks, or just pushed and piled into huge, higgledy-piggledy heaps.

Loaded trucks come snorting in, and empty trucks go rattling out. Big, cheery men go striding around, shouting and laughing and working. Everywhere hubbub and din, and a rich mixture of smells.

BENJAMIN COLLEY

In a railed-off corner of this huge market building, Benjamin Colley had a nice little vegetable business. He would buy from the farmers—who brought their goods to town— a truckload of pumpkins, or half a load of carrots; and sell them again, in smaller lots, to the greengrocers who came to stock their shops, weighing out the vegetables on his great, clanking scales.

Built up on posts above his stall, and reached by a steep and narrow ladder, was a small, square room Ben called his office. In it were a desk, a chair and an old settee, and a little pile of books: one or two stories, a worn school atlas and a dictionary, "to tell me what the words mean," he said. He was very fond of words, was Ben.

Ben loved the bustle of the market and its wonderful mixture of smells. But sometimes when his work was done he did feel a little bit lonely, and often he was bothered by the rats.

Oh, those rats! When Benjamin Colley went home to his lodgings in Woolloomooloo, when the doors were locked and the lights switched off, and only the street lamps glimmered dimly through the dusty windows, the rats came creeping wickedly out of their holes.

Nibbling at this, and gnawing at that, they chewed great holes in the vegetable sacks and bit off the tips of the juiciest carrots.

"Gormandizers!" said Ben. "Means they eat too much," said he.

And then, one day, Ben found an advertisement in his morning paper:

FOR SALE: Carpet Snake. Guaranteed non-venomous. Good ratter. Would make an affectionate and undemanding pet.

"Well now, that's an idea," said Ben. "Might fix both my troubles at once." He read it again.

"Non-venomous. Means it wouldn't bite me. At least, means if it did bite me, I wouldn't die of it. Nor my customers neither, and that's a point, too. Affectionate. Means it'd get fond of me; that'd be nice. And undemanding. Means it wouldn't ask for much — except rats. And there's plenty of those," said Ben.

So Ben bought his carpet snake and carried it back to the market in a sack slung over his shoulder. Up the ladder he went, into his office,

latching the door behind him, and tipped out the snake, like a bagful of carrots, on to the old shabby settee.

And there it stayed, for three whole days, sulking. Ben did his best to make friends and fed it on good, fresh meat, chopped into rat-sized chunks. "Affectionate, that's what you're supposed to be," said Ben. "Trouble is," said Ben, "you haven't a name. Now listen, snake. I can't go on for ever saying 'Listen, snake' and 'Here, snake' and 'Good morning, snake.' You must have a name. But none of your Tom, Dick and Harry sort of names. What about Archibald, or Algernon? Or Rutherford, or Montmorency?" The carpet snake shuddered and turned its face against the wall.

"Or a real Australian name," said Ben. "An Aboriginal name, like Nemarluk, or Jaggamara? After all, you're a native yourself. No good? Well, here's an idea. You're a carpet snake, and the best carpets come from Persia. They call places after people; why not call people after places?" He reached for the atlas and turned to the Persia page, and there it was. "Bandar Sharpur. And Sharpur for short. How's that?" said Ben.

Sharpur, the carpet snake, slithered off the settee and rubbed his cheek gently against Ben's arm. "That's more the sort of thing. Affectionate," said Ben.

"There'll be rats for your supper tonight," he told the snake. "If you can catch them, that is. And that's what you're here for. 'Good ratter,' the newspaper said."

Late that night, when the doors were locked and the lights were out, Ben brought Sharpur down the ladder, to lie still as a rope on the dusty floor, while Ben crouched in a shadowy corner to see what would happen.

Soon there was a squeaking and a scampering, and around a sack of potatoes popped a big, fat rat. It stopped, suddenly, sniffing danger.

"Glup!" said Sharpur; and the rat was gone. All that was left was a rather restless lump a little way down his neck.

Another rat came . . . and vanished. And another . . . Until Sharpur closed his eyes and settled himself down for sleep.

"Satiated," said Ben. "Means he's had enough."

Now, every night before Ben went home, he let out the carpet snake, to slide and slither and glide around the dark, shadowy market, among the sacks and the crates and the piled-up hills of pumpkins, hunting for his supper and growing fatter and sleeker week by week.

And very early every morning, Ben put Sharpur back in the office and carefully latched the door. There he slept all day, coiled like a Catherine wheel on Ben's settee, while down below him trucks snorted and roared, men shouted and laughed, and the big, brass scales clanged and rattled and bumped under their loads of marrows and beans.

But, just once, Ben forgot to turn the latch, and right in the busiest middle of the morning rush, Sharpur pushed open the door and came slithering down the ladder to look at the world below.

Well! What a commotion! "Snake, snake!" shouted one greengrocer. "Help, help!" shouted another. "Shoot it!" shouted a third.

Sharpur draped himself over a railing, like a fire hose hung up to dry, and gazed around him, happily wondering why all the fuss.

Frightened men scrambled away from him.

Braver men struggled to get at him. And one greengrocer's wife, who had come with her husband in his truck, fought her way out of the market, screaming like a fire engine all the way up Hay Street, down George Street, along Circular Quay and on to the Manly ferry.

"Pandemonium!" said Ben. "Means too much muddle and noise."

And he shouted at the top of his voice, much louder than anyone else, "There's . . . no . . . need . . . to panic! It's only Sharpur, my carpet snake. Guaranteed non-venomous. My affectionate and undemanding pet. Gentlemen, meet Sharpur. Sharpur, meet the gentlemen."

Then everyone was very ashamed of being so scared; but no one felt really happy until Sharpur was back in the office, with the door securely latched.

That very same afternoon, the Board that controlled the market held an Extraordinary General Meeting, and Ben was told to attend.

"Sharpur will have to go," said the Chairman. "We can't have snakes in the market."

"But — guaranteed non-venomous," pleaded Ben.

"We can't help that," said the Chairman. "*You* know he's non-venomous, and *we* know he's non-venomous, and it'd be quite all right in a country warehouse, where everybody knows about carpet snakes. But we *can't* have snakes in the *city*."

"I'd be lonely without him," said Ben. "He's my affectionate —"

"We wouldn't want to be hard," interrupted the Chairman. "We'll give you a week. At the end of a week, either Sharpur must go, or you both must go."

"It'll have to be both," Ben told Sharpur. "I couldn't stay here without you. Wherever we go, we'll go together. But I'll certainly miss the market. I've lived all my life in the city, and what will I do in the bush?"

The week was slipping away and would soon be gone, and the news was spreading around the market. The fruit and vegetable men were talking it over.

"It's a pity about that snake," said one. "It wasn't his fault the people were scared. I'd be sorry to see him go."

"It's a pity about Ben Colley," said somebody else. "He's a shy sort of quiet chap, but everyone likes him."

"It's a pity about us too, if Sharpur goes," said a wise old potato merchant. "Remember the rats? We'd better talk to the Chairman." So off they all went to the Board Room.

"Well, do you know, I'd forgotten about the rats," the Chairman said when they told him. "I've hardly seen any about since Sharpur's been here."

He thought for a while, and he thought a bit more, and at last he said, "You'd better tell Benjamin Colley I'm giving him one more chance . . . BUT . . . you must put up a notice," he said.

"ANY CARPET SNAKE seen in this building is for keeping down the rats, and is hereby guaranteed to be absolutely non-venomous."

43

Ben was delighted, and quite astonished to find he had so many friends, all shaking his hand and patting his back and wishing him well. "I needn't have ever been lonely," said Ben. "Just wait till I run and tell Sharpur."

He raced up the ladder and into the office, where Sharpur lay fast asleep on the old settee.

"Exonerated!" shouted Ben. "Means it wasn't your fault, and they're letting you off."

Sharpur opened one sleepy eye and yawned: a deep, enormous, wide-open, cavernous yawn. Then he closed his eye again. He was pleased, of course, but Ben could tell him about it some other time. After all, it was midday.

"And midday," thought Sharpur, "is a time
for sleep."